OWLKIDS BOOKS

Rock? Plant? Animal?

How Nature Keeps Us Guessing

WRITTEN BY **Etta Kaner** | ILLUSTRATED BY **Brittany Lane**

Are you a nature detective? Can you tell the difference between a **rock**, a **plant**, and an **animal**? Sometimes it's easy, but sometimes it's not!

HERE ARE SOME CLUES:

A **rock** is a solid, nonliving thing that is made up of one or more minerals. Minerals are found in the earth. The color of a rock depends on the minerals in it.

A **plant** is a living thing that grows in one spot and makes its own food using sunlight. Plants usually have roots, stems, and leaves. They are often green, but not always!

An **animal** is a living being. Animals use their bodies to move around. Some eat other animals to survive, some eat only plants, and some eat both.

Look closely at this picture. Do you think this is a **rock**, a *plant*, or an ***animal***?

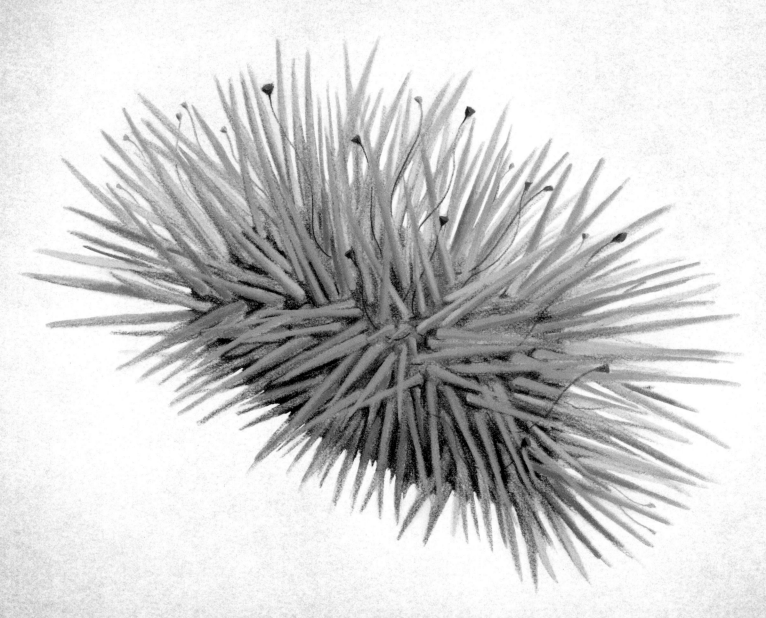

TURN THE PAGE TO FIND OUT THE ANSWER!

It's an ANIMAL!

This purple sea urchin lives in the ocean. What might look like spiky flower petals are really spines! The urchin uses them for catching food. The spines also protect the urchin from *most* of its predators, though sea otters don't seem to mind them. In fact, some sea otters eat so many urchins that their teeth are stained purple!

But animals aren't the only things in nature that might not look like what you expect. There are plants and even some rocks that can fool you, too!

See if you can guess what you are looking at in this book ... Is it a rock? A plant? An animal? You just might be surprised!

Rock? Plant? Animal?

ANIMAL!
This is a *reef stonefish*.

If you swam along the sea bottom, you'd probably miss this rock-shaped fish. It spends most of its time motionless, blending in with its surroundings. But when another fish happens by, watch out! The stonefish swallows it whole ten times faster than you blink your eyes. And predators are no match for it either. The stonefish has thirteen spines along its back that can stand upright and shoot out venom when it's threatened.

Rock? Plant? Animal?

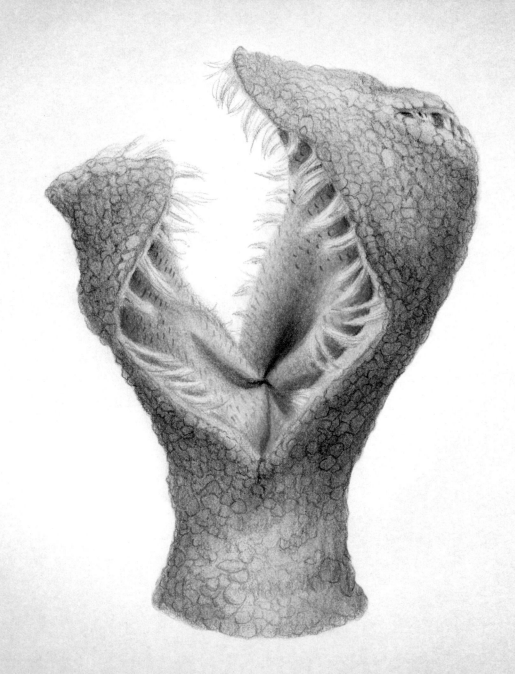

PLANT!
This is a *jackal food plant*.

Do you think it would be easy to catch sight of this bright orange, toothy-looking flower? It's not! This plant grows mostly underground. The flower bud breaks through the soil only after many heavy rains. This can take several years to happen because it's very dry where the jackal food plant lives. If you do come across it, don't get too close. It won't bite, but it does smell like poop!

Rock? Plant? Animal?

ANIMAL!
This is a *leafy sea dragon*.

Unlike most fish, the leafy sea dragon is a poor swimmer. So how does it stay safe from predators if it can't get away quickly? It uses its leafy camouflage to hide. By living among seaweed and seagrass, and swaying its body back and forth like a water plant, a leafy sea dragon makes itself hard to spot. It can even change color to match its seaweed habitat!

Rock? Plant? Animal?

PLANT!
This is a *cobra lily*.

Just like a real cobra, the cobra lily has a forked tongue. Only this plant's "tongue" is a long, leafy part covered with sweet nectar. Insects looking for a sweet treat land on the tongue and follow the nectar to an opening in the lily. Once inside, the insects fall to the bottom and drown in a special liquid that helps the plant digest its food. Mmm ... cobra lily lunch is now being served!

Rock? Plant? Animal?

ROCK!
These are *dendrites*.

Dendrites are branch-like rock patterns that form inside rocks. Dendrites start off as just a few tiny crystals of a mineral called manganese. Over thousands of years, more and more crystals form and become these beautiful, delicate shapes. A similar thing happens when frost crystals grow on your windows in winter, only those develop much more quickly!

Rock? Plant? Animal?

ANIMAL!
This is an *orchid mantis*.

To other insects, the orchid mantis looks just like a yummy, nectar-filled flower. In fact, some bees and butterflies prefer the large, colorful mantis to the real flowers growing nearby. But little do those insects know that *they* will become the mantis' lunch if they get too close. With lightning speed, the mantis grabs the prey with its front legs and digs in with its tiny teeth.

Rock? Plant? Animal?

PLANT!

This is an *ant plant*.

This plant's brown, swollen stem might look like a rock, but it acts like a hotel for the ants that live inside it. Tiny dots along its leaves are filled with nectar that the ants eat. In exchange for a safe home and food, the ants defend the plant by stinging any other insects or birds that try to eat it. And another bonus for having these ants as guests? Their poop provides nutrients that help the plant grow!

Rock? Plant? Animal?

ANIMAL!
This is a *red feather star*.

You won't see a fernlike feather star on any forest floor. Instead, it can be found in the ocean. When it's resting, a red feather star curls up into a bowl shape. But when it's time to eat, it uncurls as many as 200 sticky arms and waves them about. Tiny plants and animals floating by are caught in its arms and become that night's dinner. Any leftovers go to the small shrimp, fish, and crabs that live on and around the feather star.

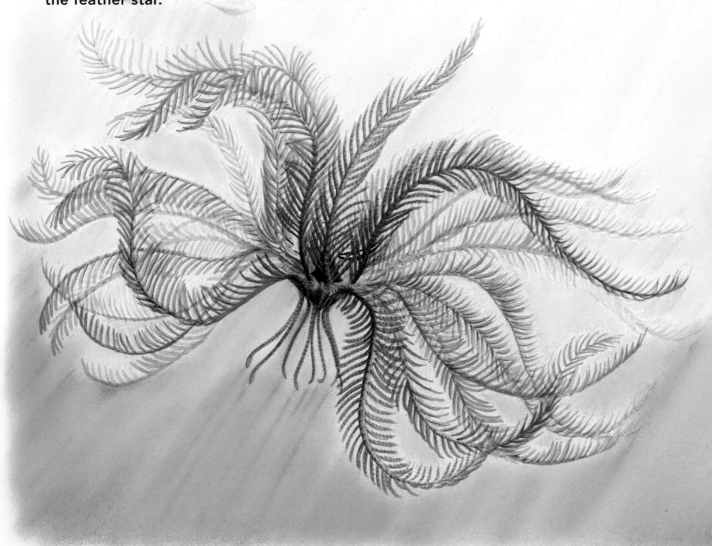

Rock? Plant? Animal?

ANIMAL!

This is a *giant green anemone*.

This giant green anemone may look like a pretty flower, but it's really a hungry hunter. As ocean currents push mussels, crabs, shrimp, and sea urchins by the anemone, it stretches out its stinging tentacles to grab and paralyze its next meal. The anemone then uses its tentacles to push its prey into its mouth. And any hard bits that aren't digested, such as empty shells, come back out this same hole. Imagine using your mouth for both eating and pooping!

Rock? Plant? Animal?

ANIMAL!
This is a *giant Malaysian leaf insect.*

When is a leaf not a leaf? When it's a giant Malaysian leaf insect. This creature not only looks like a leaf but moves like one, too! Instead of scurrying like most insects, it walks very slowly. Then when it stops, it moves its body and legs back and forth to look like a leaf blowing in the wind. Predators are fooled into thinking it is just a leaf rather than a tasty insect, so they pass it by.

Rock? Plant? Animal?

ROCK!
This is a *desert rose*.

These "roses" are actually rocks that took up to 250 million years to form! Most desert roses are made of two kinds of minerals: mainly barite and some quartz. Both of these minerals form as crystals. The barite crystals have the shape of rose petals, which is what gives the desert roses their flowery look!

Rock? Plant? Animal?

PLANT!
This is a *lithops plant*.

Although these might look like stones, they are really the tips of leaves. The rest of the lithops plant is underground, out of the hot desert sun. But like all plants, it uses the sun's energy to help make the food it needs. So how does the plant catch the sun's rays if it's mostly underground? The wax paper-thin top layers of the leaves act like windows. They allow light to shine through to reach the rest of the plant below.

ANIMAL!

This is a *satanic leaf-tailed gecko*.

If you see a brown leaf hanging from a tree in the Madagascar rain forest, you might want to look again. It could actually be a satanic leaf-tailed gecko. With a body covered in leaflike veins and splotches that look like moss, this small reptile easily fools predators. The only giveaway might be the flash of its bright red tongue. The gecko doesn't have eyelids, so it uses its tongue like a windshield wiper to clean its eyes.

Were you surprised by some of the ROCKS, PLANTS, and ANIMALS in this book?

In nature, things aren't always what they seem at first glance. And this is also true with one specific animal—humans! You can't tell what a person is like just by the way they look. You need to get to know them.

Now that you know that there's often more than meets the eye, it's time to explore your world more closely!

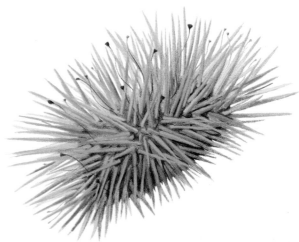

Words to Know

CRYSTAL:
a solid formation that takes the shape of a repeating pattern

HABITAT:
a place where a plant or animal lives

MINERAL:
a solid substance that makes up rocks, sand, and soil

NECTAR:
a sweet liquid made by flowers

NUTRIENT:
a substance in food that helps bodies grow and stay healthy

PREDATOR:
an animal that eats other animals

PREY:
an animal that is eaten by other animals

RAIN FOREST:
a forest that receives a lot of rain yearly

TENTACLE:
a thin, flexible body part that sticks out around the mouth or head of an animal and is used for feeling, moving, or grasping

For my darling David, an inspiration to us all—E.K.

For Ian, always my rock—B.L.

ACKNOWLEDGMENTS: Thank you to Raymond McDougall, Kevin Downy, and David K. Joyce for the rock and mineral mentoring, and to Larry Hodgson for his insights into plants. A huge thanks to Brittany Lane for her amazing artwork, to Alisa Baldwin for her imaginative design, and to Stacey Roderick, editor extraordinaire. What a team!

Owlkids Books acknowledges the financial support of the Canada Council for the Arts, the Ontario Arts Council, the Government of Canada through the Canada Book Fund (CBF) and the Government of Ontario through the Ontario Creates Book Initiative for our publishing activities.

Owlkids Books gratefully acknowledges that our office in Toronto is located on the traditional territory of many nations, including the Mississaugas of the Credit, the Chippewa, the Wendat, the Anishinaabeg, and the Haudenosaunee Peoples.

Published in Canada by Owlkids Books Inc., 1 Eglinton Avenue East, Toronto, ON M4P 3A1
Published in the US by Owlkids Books Inc., 1700 Fourth Street, Berkeley, CA 94710

Library of Congress Control Number: 2021951242

Library and Archives Canada Cataloguing in Publication

Title: Rock? Plant? Animal? : how nature keeps us guessing / written by Etta Kaner ; illustrated by Brittany Lane.
Names: Kaner, Etta, author. | Lane, Brittany, illustrator.
Identifiers: Canadiana 20210377038 | ISBN 9781771474443 (hardcover)
Subjects: LCSH: Mimicry (Biology)—Juvenile literature.
Classification: LCC QH546 .K36 2022 | DDC j578.4—dc23

Edited by Stacey Roderick | Designed by Alisa Baldwin

MIX
Paper | Supporting responsible forestry
FSC® C010256
www.fsc.org

Manufactured in Shenzhen, Guangdong, China, in August 2023, by WKT Co. Ltd.
Job # 23CB1432

hc   B   C   D   E   F   G

Publisher of Chirp, Chickadee and OWL
www.owlkidsbooks.com

Owlkids Books is a division of  bayard canada